Speaking Our Faith Leader Guide

Equipping the Next Generations to Tell the Old, Old Story

KIT CARLSON

Church Publishing
NEW YORK

Church Publishing Incorporated
Editorial Offices
19 East 34th Street
New York, NY 10016

Cover design by: Jennifer Kopec, 2 Pug Design
Typeset by: PerfecType, Nashville, TN
Printed in the United States of America

A record of the book is available from the Library of Congress.

ISBN: 978-1-64065-029-9 (pbk.)
ISBN: 978-1-64065-030-5 (ebook)

To Andrew and Katie

Contents

Introduction   7

Session One: Setting the Tone   21

Session Two: How Do You Know What You Know?   27

Session Three: Who Is the God That We Know?   31

Session Four: Faith in Action: Practices and Ethics   34

Session Five: This I Believe   39

The Final Celebration: One Month Later   44

Handouts   49

Introduction

Episcopalians, we're not God's "frozen chosen." We're God's introverted people. And we're kind of shy and polite. But most of what we tend to be as a church . . . we're not pushy people. That's not our way, and I don't think we need to pretend to be that. We need to be who we are. God's shy people need to share their stories in ways that are authentic to them and that matter.

—Presiding Bishop Michael Curry, speaking to Episcopal
Communicators on April 21, 2016

Speaking about faith does not come naturally or easily to many people, particularly people who have been raised and nurtured in the Episcopal Church or another mainline Protestant denomination. The practice of evangelism has not been emphasized in our traditions. It too often seems to be the province of other sorts of Christianity, the sorts of Christianity that tend to make "God's shy people" very uncomfortable.

But there is a fresh wind blowing through our church, as Episcopalians begin to answer Presiding Bishop Michael Curry's call to join the Jesus Movement, the movement of love and reconciliation and justice that Jesus began on the shores of the Sea of Galilee, and that has poured out through the ages wherever people are working to change the world—as Bishop Curry says—"from the nightmare it often is into the dream that God intends." Part of that Jesus Movement is to bring people into deeper relationship with the loving, liberating, life-giving God whom we follow.

And that means that a significant aspect of the Jesus Movement is evangelism—telling the Good News, the "old, old story of Jesus and his love,"[1] as the old hymn puts it. "God's shy people" are going to need to warm up and get more comfortable with speaking about their faith, their love of God, and their passion for Jesus and his Way. "God's shy people" are going to need to be able to respond with a whole-hearted "yes" to Bishop Curry's summons: "Now is our time to go. To go into the

---

1. Hymn 64 in *Lift Every Voice and Sing II*.

world to share the Good News of God and Jesus Christ. To go into the world and help to be agents and instruments of God's reconciliation. To go into the world, let the world know that there is a God who loves us, a God who will not let us go, and that that love can set us all free."[2]

"God's shy people" are going to need to learn to put words to their faith, to "always be ready to make your defense to anyone who demands from you an accounting for the hope that is in you" (1 Pet. 3:15). But this is not going to happen automatically or without preparation. If "God's shy people" are going to be able to share their stories in ways that are authentic to them and that matter, as Bishop Curry said, then they are going to need to get comfortable talking about faith, comfortable sharing their stories, and comfortable listening to the faith stories of other people.

That is why I developed Speaking Our Faith. Initially, I created it as a project to use with younger adults—people under age forty—to see if they could be better equipped to talk about faith with people their own age who did not share their faith. But it proved to be so transformative with those first participants, that other, older people in my congregation wanted a chance to try Speaking Our Faith, too. I trained five lay members of my parish to facilitate these groups and currently, more than eighty people in my church have participated in Speaking Our Faith. In the process, they got more comfortable speaking about faith. But they also found their faith renewed, and many of them became more engaged in the life and work of the church as a result. They got excited and joined the Jesus Movement.

This leader guide will help you to do the same thing, to help "God's shy people" get more comfortable speaking about faith. It is rooted in a series of five small-group conversational sessions, followed by a final gathering a month after the fifth session. In between the fifth session and the final gathering, participants are encouraged to go out and have a conversation about faith with someone they know who does not share their faith. Not an attempt at conversion, not a sales pitch, but an authentic interchange with someone they already have a relationship with. Just to talk, to listen, to share—person to person, heart to heart—something about their life with God, their walk with Jesus, or their life in a faith

---

2. "Presiding Bishop Michael Curry: This is the Jesus Movement, and we are The Episcopal Church, the Episcopal branch of Jesus' movement in this world," The Public Affairs Office, The Episcopal Church, November 2, 2015. www.episcopal church.org/posts/publicaffairs/presiding-bishop-michael-curry-jesus-movement -and-we-are-episcopal-church (accessed June 1, 2017).

community. To give them their first taste of real evangelism—which is simply talking, sharing Good News, passing on the love of Jesus.

While Speaking Our Faith is a small-group experience (and may be a perfect starting place if you want to begin a small-group ministry in your church), it is not a class, like *Alpha* or a Bible study. The knowledge that gets shared in these groups comes from the participants themselves. As they engage in a series of conversations, listening deeply to one another and sharing honestly, participants embark on a journey of constructive theology. Constructive theology is a way of thinking about God that approaches theology, not as a system of doctrines to be learned, but as a way of building a theology that engages with the world we inhabit. If a person's set of beliefs are like "a landscape—a vast and complex terrain holding within its borders all those images, stories, concepts, practices, and feelings that make up the sum total of 'what we believe in,'"[3] then the Speaking Our Faith approach helps participants become theological map makers. By wrestling honestly with what they do and do not believe, and by hearing how others wrestle with their own faith, participants begin to make sense of faith . . . *their own faith*, as it has been taught by the church, formed by their life experiences, and owned and understood in their own hearts and minds.

As the group leader, it is your sacred task to lead them on this journey through their vast and complex landscapes of faith. It requires sensitive listening on your part, the ability to facilitate a group conversation so that every person can participate fully, and nonjudgmental respect for each participant's understandings and questions around God, Jesus, Spirit, church, life, the universe, and everything. But the group members themselves do the real work. It is really their own honesty, vulnerability, and willingness to participate that will make Speaking Our Faith a transformative experience for everyone. Your job is just to help them stay on the path, through a series of guided conversations that lead them, in the end, to the creation of a personal statement of faith. And then, of course, to the final challenge: having a conversation about faith with someone they know who does not share their faith.

This guide provides the template for hosting these "sacred conversations." It begins with the personal preparations you need to make as the group leader, in order to facilitate conversations that will free the

---

3. Serene Jones and Paul Lakeland, eds., *Constructive Theology: A Contemporary Approach to Classical Themes with CD-ROM* (Minneapolis: Fortress Press, 2005), 9.

participants to put words to the faith that is in them. Then the five conversation sessions are fully outlined. They begin with a session that really helps the group members to get to know one another and to feel secure sharing their stories with one another. The sessions continue, beginning with the basic question of theology: how do we know what we know, and how do we know it is God? They move through basic theological ideas—who is the God that we know, and what are the qualities of that God? And then to questions of ethics and practices—how is one to live in relationship with this God?

The final session is the presentation of participants' own statements of faith, their own articulation of what they believe about God and what is required of them as a person who follows and worships this God. Finally, the group is gathered together again after several weeks apart to reconnect, and to report on the outcomes of the conversations about faith that they were able to have with others. In between the sessions, participants have exercises to work on at home.

As you enroll members for your group, please be sure they are willing to commit to the entire process. This includes five weeks of ninety-minute conversation sessions, the exercises in between sessions, and the final gathering. To have conversations at this depth, and to feel safe enough to speak and share honestly, participants need to be able to count on one another to show up and to engage fully.

"God's shy people" have been quietly faithful for a long time. To come out of their shells and speak about faith is a process. It doesn't happen quickly, but it can in fact happen. This may be the first step in a person's journey to evangelism, to being able to "tell the old, old story of Jesus and his love." The love and fellowship of Jesus that they experience in their Speaking Our Faith group can make all the difference in their willingness to step out and speak about that love and fellowship with others. Bless you, as a leader on this Speaking Our Faith journey, and may you find grace and transforming love in this process.

Facilitating Sacred Conversations

A Speaking Our Faith group is not like a typical church small group, where people might gather for Bible study and prayer, or for discussion about a book or a video. These conversations are meant to be less spontaneous, and more thoughtful and intentional. While people may laugh, joke, and connect to things someone else has said, it's not a space where people debate conflicting ideas or theologies or talk over one another, or think harder about what they are going to say next than about the words that someone else is speaking.

If you are trained in one of the many current methods of facilitating deep conversations—Appreciative Inquiry, The Circle Way, World Café, The Art of Hosting, and the like—you will already understand the principles that make for a rich conversation. In my own work in the church, I have used these methods in various settings, so I applied these techniques and practices when I developed Speaking Our Faith. And one thing I learned as I developed this program—these groups are *not* discussion groups. They are conversation groups. And understanding the difference between the two is crucial.

A discussion group:

- Meets to share ideas, reactions, and plans, as in a Bible study or a regular church meeting.
- May be highly energetic, with people leaning in, jumping on top of each other's sentences, and with a few people who are more extroverted and engaged leading the way.
- May surface opposing viewpoints, with participants vigorously defending their own positions.
- Often works at a "head" level, not a "heart" level.

In contrast, a conversation group:

- Relies on full participation from all the members of the group, regardless of whether they are introverted or extroverted, outgoing or shy.
- Emphasizes deep and respectful listening to one another, as much as speaking.
- Seeks common ground, while accepting differences.
- The facilitator may lead, but the group owns the responsibility for the success of the conversation.
- Allows space for meaning to emerge, often tapping into deeper emotions, convictions, and values than a more "heady" discussion might do.

So, to prepare to facilitate a conversation—rather than to lead a discussion—you will need to move intentionally through a series of stages: knowing yourself and knowing your group; creating a container for conversation; asking questions and honoring answers with intention; keeping your eyes, ears, and heart open.

Knowing Yourself and Knowing Your Group

Who are you, and who are the people in the group you are about to convene? Speaking Our Faith groups have been offered in many different constellations of leaders and participants. My original group was a mix of younger Christians under age forty. I was the pastor and priest for some of them, but not all. Most of them were Episcopalians, but a few joined in from other faith traditions—Presbyterian, Lutheran, and evangelical. They were students, parents, teachers, and private sector employees. They did not all know each other well prior to this Speaking Our Faith group, but they all entered the group willing to participate fully in the process.

After the success of that first group, I trained leaders in my congregation to lead Speaking Our Faith, and they convened groups of fellow parishioners of a variety of ages and life experiences. Some of these groups bonded tightly—one, a group of young mothers, continues to meet monthly. Others struggled to jell. As I shared Speaking Our Faith more widely, it has been used by a rector with a vestry, by a college chaplain with students, by a volunteer with a group of assisted-living residents. Each group has its own personality. So does each facilitator.

So, begin with some self-reflection on your part. Why are you facilitating this group? What is your objective—to make evangelists, to build stronger small groups in your church, to crack the "politeness barrier" in your congregation and get into a deeper level of dialogue? What do you hope will happen, and what do you fear will happen? Do you like people and enjoy hearing their stories? What pushes your own buttons when you are in a church group? What can you draw upon in your previous experiences leading or facilitating a group, and what do you think you still need to learn?

And it's important to get to know the members of your group, too. Even if you are in a small church, and you think everyone in your group knows everyone else, you will be surprised at what you learn from people you may have known your whole life, once you start having these conversations. So about two weeks before your group meets for the first time, send its members this "getting to know you" email.

Dear <Name>,

I am so excited to begin the Speaking Our Faith sessions with you and the rest of our group on <date>. To help me guide our conversations better, I'd like to know a little bit about you and where you are on your journey of faith right now. Could you answer the following questions in a reply to me? Thanks, and I will see you soon.

In Christ's peace,
<Your Name>

1. Say something about your current state of faith, where you are in your relationship with Jesus and with the church.
2. Do you talk about your faith with other people? If you do, who do you talk to and under what sorts of conditions? What do you say?
3. If you don't, what do you wish you could say to someone else about your relationship with God? What would you prefer to keep to yourself?
4. What strengthens your ability to speak about your own relationship with God?
5. What hinders your ability to speak about your own relationship with God?

And some basic information . . .
Age:
Ethnicity/national origin:
Gender and gender identity:
Educational level attained:
Were you raised in a family that practiced a religious faith? If so, which one?
Current denominational affiliation, if any:

As their replies come in, keep these emails in a safe and confidential location. I like to print them out and put them in a large envelope or manila folder, and then during my daily prayer time in the days before a group begins, I re-read their responses and pray for each group member. It is transformative to pray daily for these people prior to the group ever getting together. When you enter the space that first day and sit down with them, they will already be familiar and beloved to you, because you have known them first in prayer.

Creating a Container for Conversation
Your primary task as group leader is to create and hold the space where the group can come alive in its conversations about faith. When

it comes to speaking about faith, I have found that three themes keep emerging: *vulnerability, not having all the answers*, and *learning to speak one's own truth*. These themes highlight the barriers to speaking about faith, as well as the joys of speaking about faith. People come to these groups with their guard up. Speaking about faith is not widely done in our tradition, and people may be hesitant for a variety of reasons. The first is that it requires a certain amount of vulnerability to share one's life and experiences with God. Our relationship with God can be intimate, intense, powerful, distant, joy-filled, a struggle, and possibly life-changing. To talk about those sorts of things requires the ability to be vulnerable. Brené Brown, well-known researcher specializing in shame and vulnerability, defines vulnerability as *uncertainty, risk*, and *emotional exposure*.[4] The members of your group may become more comfortable with one another over time, but please remember that at the outset they are opening themselves up in ways that may feel unfamiliar and even dangerous to them. The group needs to be a safe place for vulnerable conversation.

One of the reasons group participants feel vulnerable is because they don't feel comfortable with *not having all the answers*. They have not been theologically trained, generally. They may have mixed feelings about the difference between the theology in their current church, versus the theology they learned in the faith or denomination they have left behind. They may believe that everyone else in the room knows exactly what it means to be a Christian, and that if they express doubts or questions, they will be exposed as an imposter. They may be struggling with their own faith and find it hard to be honest about that struggle. They may be embarrassed by the speech of other kinds of Christians in the world, and while they know they don't believe *that*, they may worry that what they *do* believe is wrong or heretical. The group needs to be able to listen and respond without judgment as people struggle with their uncertainty and confusion.

And finally, the group process can lead people to the point where they are able to *speak their own truth*. But it's not realistic to expect that people are ready to speak their own perfectly realized faith statements in the very first week. The process of conversation, conducted

---

4. Brené Brown, *Daring Greatly: How the Courage to Be Vulnerable Transforms the Way We Live, Love, Parent, and Lead* (New York: Gotham, 2012), 34.

with trustworthy people in a safe space, can lead people to greater ability at speaking about God and faith. But they may be halting, hesitant, and unsure at first, because this is an unfamiliar experience for them.

As leader, you help the group construct the norms and guidelines that will create a strong holding environment for their conversation. In the first session, much of the time is spent on introductions, exploratory questions, and the setting of norms for the group. Good norms are especially important in creating a safe space for conversation. The group should develop its norms under your guidance, and every week when you gather again, review the norms, and check in with your group to be sure everyone remembers the guidelines the group established and is still willing to honor them.

Your leadership in conversation will also help to create the holding environment. You must model the kind of speaking and listening that you want the group members to practice. When someone is speaking, give them your full attention, without peeking to see what the next question is that you might want to ask. When someone finishes, say things like, "Thank you for sharing that." Or, "what do other people think?" Or, "was that hard or easy for you to say?" Practice respectful listening and respectful speaking. Also help the group to maintain its own norms. If someone tries to cut in, gently remind them that "X has not finished speaking yet." Then when person X finishes, turn to the interrupter and ask, "Was there something you wanted to add to this?" Think of yourself as a conductor of the conversation, drawing out the shy folks, muting the more talkative folks, honoring the words that are said, and all the time moving the conversation forward and deeper as you go. If the group members feel secure in your leadership, they will feel safe enough to open up with one another.

And even the environment of your meeting space helps to create the container. It should be a place where confidential conversation can be safely held. So probably not a local coffee shop or pub, but maybe the usual church classroom or meeting room. Or the living room of your own home, or a group member's home—if family members and pets aren't continually wandering through the space. Will you feel more comfortable sitting around a table, or in an open circle of chairs or sofas? You can also put a focal image in the center of your circle, like a candle or icon, a bowl of water, or a photograph. This gives you all something to look at that can refocus attention that starts to wander.

Asking Questions and Honoring Answers with Intention

The process of Speaking Our Faith is like a guided group interview. Each session frames the questions of faith in a different light. The questions provided for the leader are meant as a road map, or a guide, to lead people through the process of talking about their faith on a specific topic. You probably won't get through all the questions in any of the sessions. The questions are there to be sure you have enough material at your disposal to guide the conversation.

When you ask the conversation questions, don't be afraid of spaces of silence. People sometimes need to get their thoughts in order before they speak. One of the longest silences I had in a group was after I asked the question, "Who is the God that you know?" Once they got past the superficially easy answers, like "God is love," there were longer and longer gaps of silence as each person really probed their own thoughts and ideas about God before they could start putting words to their beliefs.

Also, be sure each person has had a chance to answer a question before you move on to the next. This means keeping track of who has not gone, even if the question sparks some interchange among group members. It's easy for the shy folks to sit quietly while others talk—and it's ok to directly ask the shy ones, "Did you want to say something about this question?" Or, "What do you think?"

Honoring group members' answers with intention means really listening to what they say, and responding in ways that affirm, go deeper, or frame the question in a more accessible way. If a person says that a certain prayer brings them closer to God, and it's also one of your favorite prayers, it's fine to tell the group that. You don't have to simply be a kind of detached interviewer. But you also don't want to dominate the conversation, either. This is their space and their time. Saying, "Thank you for sharing that," is also always a good affirmation. Reminding them that what this person is saying connects to what another person said in an earlier conversation can let them know you are hearing what's being said, and also help them to hear one another better.

You may have to be creative in your questioning. In the conversation about "who is the God that you know?", I had to frame the question three different ways to get the group to really dig in to the topic. First, I said, "I thought today we might talk about, not what we don't know about God, but what you *do* know about God out of your own experience and life and knowledge." That generated the series of short answers with long silences in between. And finally, Mike, one of the participants, said, "You're almost asking for our personal theologies that we've built up, and I don't know if I could define them quickly, or easily, or clearly even."

So, I tried another approach: "That's why I was interested in what was the first thing out of everybody's mouth, because that's where we start from, right? So, what else might one say about God?" They continued to struggle, not really able to answer the question. So I reworded the question again: "Maybe another way to get at it is *who* is the God you pray to. So, what's the nature, the qualities of the God you pray to?" That way of wording the question finally opened up the conversation, and they really began to explore their ideas about God. So the session questions in this guide may not necessarily work as written with your group. You may need to rework, reword, and rethink what is being asked to help your group to explore the topic. The important task is to facilitate your own group's exploration. Don't be afraid to improvise.

Keeping Your Eyes, Ears, and Heart Open

Everybody has a story. And everyone is in the midst of a human life, which is their own personal drama of love and loss, joy and sorrow, despair and redemption. As group leader, you need to keep that notion of story—life as personal drama—in the back of your mind at all times. The participants may come wanting to share their thoughts about God, but they may be coming from a hard family situation, a struggle at work, or the stress of a job interview. While you don't want the stories to overwhelm the conversation, as group leader, you will also know those stories are lurking under the surface, and they may need to emerge from time to time. If they do, try to connect where those personal stories intersect with the discussion you are having that day, so you don't get too far off the track. What *does* that hard family situation have to do with a loving God? How *does* your relationship with Jesus get you through the struggle at work? How *might* the Holy Spirit sustain you during the stress of the job interview?

This is part of keeping your eyes, ears, and heart open to the group. Being aware of the emotional process going on among group members is important. Observe if someone seems unduly quiet or on edge that day. Divert the discussion if it gets heated or personal. Remind the group of the norms it established, if necessary. Also, pay attention to the person who looks like they want to say something, but who hasn't jumped in yet. As leader, you can invite them to share and draw them out. You are listening to what is *not* being said, even as you are listening to what is *actually* being said. It's like having two sets of ears: one for the ongoing conversation, and one for the silent conversation beneath it, the one that is expressed in body language, tone of voice, and level of engagement.

What if one or more group member doesn't participate appropriately? Not everyone is perfect, and not every group is perfect, and in the life of the church it is possible that you can have that cranky, obstructionist, self-focused, disagreeable person (and I'm sure some particular person came to mind as you read those words) sign on to be part of your group. So, what will you do with that person? You can't change people. But as leader, you can set the standards for conversation in your group.

Your first set of standards is in the group norms developed in the first session. Review them at each session. Refer to them if someone starts to push the boundaries, and remind the group that these are the standards for behavior that you all agreed to. You can ask the group to take time reworking and renegotiating the norms if they seem to need to be strengthened.

You also set standards by how you respond to the members when they speak. Telling someone that "X wasn't finished talking yet. Let's give her a chance to finish her thought," when that person begins to interrupt, reminds the whole group that the goal is for everyone to be able to speak fully and freely. If a participant says something that seems odd or out of place, you can use follow-up questions: "Why do you bring that up now?" Or, "Would you like to unpack that a little more for us? I'm not sure I understand what you mean." Or, "How does that connect to the question we're discussing?" If you are a layperson leading this group, and you feel like you are getting out of your depth, please share your concerns with your clergy person. If you are clergy, and you have a group member who is seriously affecting the group's ability to function, you may have to set a private appointment with that person to share your concerns. Don't let one person ruin this experience for the rest of the group.

But I also encourage you to give even the "hard case" person the benefit of the doubt. With a strong holding environment for conversation, that person might open up in ways you had never imagined. Remember, they also are afraid of being vulnerable, and often the prickly surface of a person is there to protect a tender soul. "Love one another as I have loved you," Jesus tells his friends. Making this group a place where the love of God can be experienced among its members is an important and basic goal of Speaking Our Faith.

Between the Sessions—Yes, There Will be Homework

When the group comes together, the participants need to have some material to draw on for their conversation. This is where the "homework" comes in. It begins with the email mentioned above. When you send this email to your group before the sessions even begin, it primes the pump. It gets them thinking about faith, talking about faith, and wondering about faith. They will have something to say the minute they enter the group, because they have been thinking about it ahead of time.

So, each session of Speaking Our Faith ends with an assignment. It is very important that your group knows up front that there will be an assignment for them to do after every session. Tell them the assignments are to expand on the topics you are discussing. Some of them are artistic, right-brained exercises. They should not fear these less-logical assignments, but give them a good try. You will find some people will love to draw their "faith as a house." Others will be completely baffled by the metaphor. Your task is to encourage them to dig into the assignment as best as they can. If nothing else, they can begin to explore why they don't want to do the assignment. Why is it difficult? What is getting in their way? What does that say about their faith life?

The group gets going at the beginning of each session by reviewing the exercises they did during their time apart.[5] In between the first and second session, participants work on their "River of Faith," the story of their lives and how God has been active in those lives. Between the second and third session, participants are supposed to choose something from their "spiritual workbench"—something that exemplifies the state of their faith right now, and bring it to share. This can be a song, a poem, a picture, or an object. Sharing these items opens up the group conversation and makes it easier to go deeper. Between the third and fourth sessions, participants are asked to draw their "house of faith." If the state of their spiritual life was a house, what would it look like? Where would

---

5. The leader is positioned as a facilitator of the group's conversations and not a full participant. Letting the time be for the group members is most important, with the facilitator taking a back seat in contributing to the conversations as much as possible.

God be present or absent? And the final assignment is for each person to write his or her own statement of faith, using the Baptismal Covenant from the Book of Common Prayer as a jumping-off point.

Finally, group members get a challenge at the end of the last session. Between the end of the last conversation and the final re-gathering celebration, each member should attempt to have a conversation about faith with someone they *already know*, but who does not share their faith. Then they get to report how that went at the reunion celebration a few weeks after Speaking Our Faith ends.

If you can be clear at the beginning about the purpose and importance of these exercises, it will help the group members to buy in to the idea. And then you will have lots of very fruitful material to work with in each session, as they share the results of their homework reflections.

With all this in mind, you are now ready to facilitate sacred conversations. So, let's dive into the meat of Speaking Our Faith: the conversation sessions.

Setting the Tone

This first session helps participants get to know one another. Establishment of group norms is an important part of this session. There is an initial round of "getting to know you" conversation, followed by explanation of the program, norm setting, and naming of expectations. Then there is a second, deeper round of "getting to know you" conversation. In this initial session, participants should begin to articulate why they decided to participate in this group, what they want other group members to know about them, and what questions they bring about God and faith as they begin this exploration.

The timer numbers at the beginning of each transition are there to help you stay on track through a ninety-minute session. Leader guidelines are offered throughout the session with questions listed below the conversation topic. Don't expect that you will get through all these suggested questions. They are there to help you guide the conversation in the best possible way for your group.

Materials Needed:
- ❏ Blank paper and markers
- ❏ Handout A: "Circles of Faith" diagram
- ❏ Handout B: "River of Life" exercise to take home
- ❏ Flip chart if you like, to record group norms

Opening Prayer   :00
(5 minutes)

Invite participants to sit comfortably, feet on the floor. Take a deep breath. Then another. Say, "We are going to sit in silence, sit in the presence of God, and pray that God's Spirit will move within and among us over these next five weeks." Hold the silence for at least five minutes. End by saying, "Now as you slowly return to the room, thank God for this time of silence and prayer." Take a pause, then say, "Amen."

Introductions   00:05
(15 minutes)

Introduce yourself first, saying a little bit about yourself, why you ended up as a leader for this group, and what you hope to gain out of leading this group. Continue with questions like these to the group:

- Who are you? What is going on in your life right now?
- Why did you decide to participate in this group? What do you hope to gain?
- What do you wonder about? Why are you here?

Creating a Safe Space   00:20
(10 minutes)

Introduce the ideas of norms by saying something like this:

- Vulnerability is an important part of speaking about your faith. This is not just about your head, what you believe in your mind. It is also about your heart, how you know and love and encounter God. In order for us to work at the level of faith, with all its questions, doubts, convictions, and joys, this should be a safe space for all of us to share freely.
- This five-week journey is designed to help you listen to God and to each other, in order to help you grow in your faith, to talk about what you know and don't know, what you believe and don't believe, what you hope for and what you fear. It will help you develop your own authentic language of faith. It will help build your confidence in talking about your faith with others. It may lead to a natural evangelism, where you are less ashamed or intimidated to talk about your relationship with God and understanding of God. But it can also lead to a deepened spiritual life, to better connections among your brothers and sisters in Christ in this church.
- There will be homework exercises between the sessions. Don't be afraid of the exercises. You may or may not like the exercise presented, but at least attempt it in faith and with a willing heart and see what comes out of it. If you have a strong resistance to the exercise, perhaps the goal for that exercise is then to explore what *is* your resistance? What bothers you about it? What are you afraid it might touch? Your willingness to engage

with the exercises and to share what comes out of them for you will enhance this experience for you and the other members of the group.

- To talk about faith like this with other people touches three main themes: vulnerability, an acceptance of not having all the answers, and the ability to speak one's own truth. The way to honor these themes and help them develop is through open-ended questions, non-judgmental listening, and open, respectful conversation.

As a leader, you might talk some about your experiences in groups like this, what you have learned about how a group can be a safe space for everyone, and about your own experiences being vulnerable in front of others. How you model these themes—your own vulnerability, your own willingness to not have all the answers, and your own ability to speak your truth—will help participants do the same.

Developing Ground Rules   00:30
(10 minutes)

Help the group to develop norms for how they are to be together. Sample norms include:

- Listen as well as you can.
- Don't jump to judgment.
- Disagree respectfully.
- It's OK to share disagreement, but not to disagree in a personal way.
- Own and articulate your own feelings.
- You can talk outside the group without identifying who said what. Strip out identifying information.
- Revisit these norms if necessary.
- No interrupting. Let each person finish his or her thought.
- Don't assume; be inquiring.
- In general, keep your phones off the table and out of your hands.

If the group has a hard time getting started, offer one or two norms off the list as a starting point. Ways to surface norms are to ask questions like: What do you need to feel comfortable in this group? What norms could help us do that? What do you need to happen to be heard? How can we help everyone be respected and heard?

The group should develop its own norms. The sample is just a sample. If the group doesn't own its own boundaries for how to be together, then people won't feel safe. After this session, prepare a list of the group's norms that you can easily refer to in future sessions—either as a handout for members, or on a sheet of flip chart paper that you post each week.

Another Round of Getting to Know You, Only Deeper   00:40
(20 minutes)

Distribute the diagram with the circles of different kinds of faith (Handout A on page 49).

- Explain how this is based on the work of John Westerhoff, who developed a model of faith formation back in the 1970s. He writes that the beginning of faith is an *experienced faith*, much like we feel as children. It's based on feelings of trust, love, and acceptance. It is basically passive, and experienced through the love of other community members.
- The next stage is *affiliative faith*. This also is based in a feeling of belonging, especially to a community with a clear identity. "In *my* church, we *always* do . . ." "Episcopalians *never* do . . ." People in this style of faith need to experience awe, wonder, and mystery.
- Growing out of this is *searching faith*. This is a time to test the community's faith story, to question and to doubt. It is a religion of head *and* heart, as the person leaves behind a noncritical acceptance of the faith they were taught and begins to wrestle with what is valid, true, and believable.
- The outer ring is *owned faith*. This is really a conversion to living a whole-hearted faith that makes a fundamental difference in the person's life. The person has wrestled with what they do and do not believe and made peace with ambiguity, while becoming clear about the purpose of belief in their own life. There may be a significant shift in behavior, in what the person spends time on and cares about, and in what they are committed to.

Open the conversation to the group members:

- Where are you on this circle?
- Where do you hope these conversations will lead you?
- What are your fears and uncertainties?

When the group has answered these questions, go around the group again and ask:

- What do you want the group to know about you going forward to help make this a valuable experience for you?

An appropriate self-disclosure of vulnerability on your part might help open this up. Start by saying something important you want the group to know about you first, that will help them understand something about where you are in your life with God. Be sure everyone has a chance to answer this question, but it is not necessary to push anybody deeper than they want to go in this first session.

River of Life Exercise   01:00
(20 minutes)

You will need blank paper and markers for everyone. If you really have twenty minutes left (sometimes conversation takes longer than you planned), then you can take your time with this. Have enough handouts of this exercise (Handout B found on page 50) for your whole group, but hold those until the end. Just give them the paper and markers to start. Read these sections below; leave some space in between them for participants to think, start to draw, etc.

THE RIVER OF LIFE EXERCISE

Begin with a blank sheet of paper. Don't draw anything yet. First, before you put anything on the paper, think briefly about the course of your whole life. If you could compare your life with a river, what would the river look like?

Leave some space and silence here . . .

When and where are the smooth, flowing waters—those times when events and relationships seem generally positive or there is a sense of ease about your life? When does the river take a sudden turn (and what caused the turn), or change from smooth waters to rough, tumbling rapids or to an excited rush of water? Are there rocks or boulders falling into your river— unexpectedly landing there, changing its direction forever? Are there points at which it flows powerfully and purposefully or seems to slow to a trickle?

Leave some space and silence here . . .

> Now, start to draw your river of life with its bends and turns, its smooth waters and rough spots, its strength/vitality, and its direction.

Leave some space . . .

> Write in your approximate age, and/or dates, along the flow of your river. Identify on your drawing the various key "marker events" in your life—the boulders in the river, or places where the river changes course—that shape your story. If you could divide your life journey into sections, where would the section divisions occur? Give names to each of the sections of your life river.

Leave some space . . .

> Now think about the various people who have accompanied you along this river's journey. What relationships have been the most significant at different points in your life? Who has most shaped you? Have there been significant losses of relationship along the way? What groups or communities of people were most important? Record these key relationships and losses in the appropriate places on your river of life. If you wish, you might also want to jot down some of the thoughts and feelings that go along with these relationships.

You will probably be running out of time at this point. Encourage participants to continue to work on their River of Life over the week ahead. Pass out the handouts at this point so they can have them as references during the time apart and for sharing at the next session.

Closing Prayer   01:20
(5 minutes)

You can develop your own closing ritual. You can use the Lord's Prayer, you can use an easily memorized prayer, or you can make a circle and ask each person to offer a short prayer or intention as you go around the circle.

Think ahead about something that feels good to you and will be routine and comfortable for the group.

How Do You Know What You Know?

This session focuses on epistemology (how you know what you know) or the question of revelation (how do you know it's God revealing God's self). By doing the "River of Life" exercise in between sessions, participants have had an opportunity to reflect on places in their life where they felt God was present or absent. This leads into a conversation about how one knows or experiences God. Where does one turn for authority in understanding these experiences? What role does a faith community play? What role does scripture play?

In this session, participants should begin to speak about how they understand and know God and what part God has played in their lives. They should also be able to talk about where they do and do not find credible authority or resources for understanding these encounters with God.

Materials Needed:

❑ List of group norms on a sheet that is easily referenced
❑ A Bible, or a copy of John 1:1–14 printed out to share among the readers
❑ River of Life homework

Opening Prayer   00:00
(10 minutes)

The Lambeth Bible study[6] is a way of encountering scripture as prayer, instead of as an objective text to be struggled with. Slowly and purposefully, someone reads the scripture. After a moment of silence, each person shares a word or phrase that stood out to them. A second person (of a different gender, if possible) reads the scripture again. This time, after a moment of silence, each person shares where the passage touches their

---

6. Also known as the *African Bible Study Method* or *Ubuntu Bible Study Method*, this was introduced by the African Delegation to the Lambeth Conference of the Anglican Church in 1998. In some ways it is similar to *Lectio Divina* (a reflective reading and praying of scriptures).

life today. Then a third person reads it again. After a moment of silence, each person shares where they hear God calling to them in this scripture to do or be something today. Use a Bible with the section marked, and pass around from reader to reader, or print out these verses before the session and pass the sheet from reader to reader.

> In the beginning was the Word, and the Word was with God, and the Word was God. He was in the beginning with God. All things came into being through him, and without him not one thing came into being. What has come into being in him was life, and the life was the light of all people. The light shines in the darkness, and the darkness did not overcome it. There was a man sent from God, whose name was John. He came as a witness to testify to the light, so that all might believe through him. He himself was not the light, but he came to testify to the light. The true light, which enlightens everyone, was coming into the world. He was in the world, and the world came into being through him; yet the world did not know him. He came to what was his own, and his own people did not accept him. But to all who received him, who believed in his name, he gave power to become children of God, who were born, not of blood or of the will of the flesh or of the will of man, but of God. And the Word became flesh and lived among us, and we have seen his glory, the glory as of a father's only son, full of grace and truth (John 1:1-14).

The three questions are:

- State one word or phrase that stands out for you.
- Where does this passage touch my life today?
- From what I've heard and shared, what is God calling me to do and be today?

River of Life Exercise   00:10
(30 minutes)

Review the "River of Life" exercise. Ask the group to take turns reflecting on:

- Who or what was God to you at the different times depicted in your diagram?

- What caused you to feel closer to, or more distant from, God at these different times?
- What places or situations were encounters with the Sacred for you?
- Have you faced situations or experiences devoid of any sense of God/the Sacred?

As you go through this session, as the leader, it's important for you to begin to "conduct" the conversation. Make sure everyone gets a chance to talk, and that a few people aren't dominating the conversation. Remember your group norms, and help the group remember them too. Listen deeply, and with compassion, and use your comments to help connect ideas and experiences between the speakers. As these sessions go on, the conversation becomes more and more the work of the group, and you as leader are the prompter, the facilitator, and the guide.

How Do We Know God?   00:40
(25 minutes)

This leads to a more open-ended conversation about how we know God, what helps us to know God and what gets in the way. The following questions can help open up the conversation. You don't have to ask them in this order, but turn to them as the conversation shifts, or lags.

- Did anything in your upbringing/religious education/church life help you to interpret these experiences of God/the Sacred?
- How do you know it was God? Did anyone or anything help you understand God's working in your life?
- What was your image of God when you were a child? a teen-ager? now?
- What has determined how you understand God? experience? church teachings? scripture? books? friendships?
- When you wonder about God, where do you seek answers/ knowledge?

Resources and Stumbling Blocks   01:05
(15 minutes)

Reading the Bible, talking about God, or attending church may be a new or unpleasant experience for your group members. Create a foundation that the group can build upon:

- Let's talk about the Bible: How has scripture informed your understanding of God?
- When is scripture helpful? When is it not helpful? What kind of authority is scripture for you in your knowledge of/relationship with God?
- What about church? Church experiences—how have they helped you know God or confused your understanding/relationship with God? What is church *for* in your life?
- What strengthens your relationship with God? What draws you closer? What opens your understanding?

Spiritual Workbench Assignment   01:20
(10 minutes)

Make a connection between today's discussion, the continuing work of the "River of Life" exercise, and next session's topic:

- When you think about your river, or your faith journey, what resources connected you to God at those key points?
- Were there books, authors, TED Talks, pop songs, hymns that were or are now important to you in your life with God? What sort of things do you have on your "spiritual workbench" that help build and strengthen your life of faith?
- Bring one of those items in next week to share with the group.

Closing Prayer   01:30
(5 minutes)

Close with the prayer practice you have developed.

Who Is the God That You Know?

This session focuses on the identity of God as each participant understands God. The "spiritual workbench" exercise is a chance for participants to reflect on things that strengthen their relationship with or understanding of God. As they share these items, the leader can begin to observe how each person understands or relates to God. What is important to them in that relationship with God comes out in the words of songs or prayers, in images or scripture verses?

Then they can begin to talk through their idea of who God is. The leader can use the three persons of the Trinity as a way to anchor the conversation and help it develop, but it is important to let the group members do their own theology as much as possible. In this session, participants become theologians, describing and questioning God and God's identity, and refining their own understandings of God as they listen to the theologies of other participants.

Materials Needed:

❑ Any audio-visual equipment to share the things participants want to offer from their "spiritual workbench"
❑ A place or area to display the offerings from the "spiritual workbench" homework
❑ *Optional:* Book of Common Prayer for each participant

Opening Prayer   00:00
(5 minutes)

Use one of the "Daily Devotions for Individuals and Families" out of the Book of Common Prayer (pp. 136–140). Another good resource is *Daily Prayer for All Seasons* (Church Publishing, 2014). Which liturgy you use depends on the time of day.

Sharing What's on Your
Spiritual Workbench   00:05
(25 minutes)

Ask each person to share what is on their "spiritual workbench." Expand the conversation about the items they brought by asking: What resources open you to God, or do you draw on to understand God or think about God? How does this help you connect to God? As each person finishes sharing, invite them to place their item on the altar/table/display place you have set up.

Who is God?   00:30
(15 minutes)

Ask:

- So, drawing on these resources, and on your whole life and experience, and on Scripture, and on what you've been taught, or what you've gleaned, what do you know about God?
- What else might one say about God?
- Who is the God to whom you pray?
- What are the nature/qualities of the God that you pray to?
- What is God never like? What must God always be like?

Note: You may choose to repeat some or all of the above questions during the discussions on both Jesus and the Holy Spirit below.

What about Jesus? How does
Jesus fit into your image of God?   00:45
(15 minutes)

- What else might one say about Jesus?

What about the Holy Spirit?   1:00
(20 minutes)

Additional questions if you have time:

- What's the relationship with God like for you? One-way/two-way? a conversation?
- When you pray, what do you hear back?
- What can be said about God as you know God?

- What is beyond saying? How can that be expressed?
- What else might one say about the Trinity?

My Faith as a House   1:20
(5 minutes)

Ask participants to think about this metaphor:

> Your faith, your life of faith, your life with God, is like a house. It has a foundation. It has walls that hold it up. It has a roof to protect it from the elements. It has spaces where you meet people. It has spaces that are extremely private. It may have spaces you have never explored before. So, think for a moment—if your faith were a house, what kind of house would it be?

Then send them out with this assignment:

- For next session, draw a house or a building that depicts your faith.
- What rooms does it have? Are there stairs, gardens, sunny spots, scary attics? What's holding it up? What's inside? What needs remodeling? What is beautiful and homey?

This can be the most challenging, and at the same time, most stimulating of the homework exercises. Assure participants that they do not need to be good at drawing. They can do as elaborate or as basic a sketch of faith-as-a-house as they want. If they absolutely cannot draw, they can come next time and give a verbal description of their house. But regardless, encourage them to give this exercise a try. It will stimulate their entire brains, and new thoughts or realizations can emerge as a result. If you have time, do this exercise for yourself ahead of time and take a few minutes here, at the end of this session, to share your own house of faith with the group—as an example and inspiration to the group as they head out into the week.

Closing Prayer   1:25
(5 minutes)

Close with the prayer practice you have developed.

Faith in Action: Practices and Ethics

This session really functions in two parts. The "house of faith" exercise requires that a certain amount of time be spent so each individual in the group can share their houses. This can be an instructive and transformative exercise for participants as they really try to sort their faith, their questions, their struggles, and areas of further growth into rooms, closets, and attics. They will want to talk about it.

As they offer their "constructions" of faith, a space is created to lead from the House of Faith into the question of practices. Because if one's faith is like this house that one has drawn, then how is one to live in this world? What practices hold up the house? What practices remodel and renovate the house? What ethics emerging from this house of faith dictate how one lives in the world?

A list of typical Christian practices (Handout C on page 53) can help people think about their faith as something one "does" as much as it is something one "believes." In this session, participants begin to align the interior aspect of their faith with the exterior aspects of their everyday lives.

Materials Needed:

❏ The Book of Common Prayer or copies of Psalm 16:5-11, one copy for each person
❏ Copies of Typical Christian Practices (Handout C)
❏ Copies of the Baptismal Covenant exercise (Handouts D and E)

Opening Prayer   00:00
(5 minutes)

Distribute copies of the Book of Common Prayer (turn to page 600) or printed copies of Psalm 16:5-11 to each person. Take a moment of centering and breathing, then go around the group, with each person reading a verse. At the end, take another moment of silence and thanksgiving and conclude by saying "Amen."

Psalm 16:5-11 (Book of Common Prayer)

[5] O LORD, You are my portion and my cup; *
it is you who uphold my lot.
[6] My boundaries enclose a pleasant land; *
indeed, I have a goodly heritage.
[7] I will bless the LORD who gives me counsel; *
my heart teaches me, night after night.
[8] I have set the LORD always before me; *
because he is at my right hand I shall not fall.
[9] My heart, therefore, is glad, and my spirit rejoices; *
my body also shall rest in hope.
[10] For you will not abandon me to the grave, *
nor let your holy one see the Pit.
[11] You will show me the path of life; *
in your presence there is fullness of joy, and in your right
        hand are pleasures for evermore.

My Faith as a House   00:05
(45 minutes)

Ask each person to present their house of faith and describe it, explaining each room and what it means to them. Follow-up questions to ask to unpack their descriptions a little more can include:

- Where is your faith grounded? How have you built it up?
- What strengthens it, keeps it upright? What threatens it? Has it withstood any storms? Which is worse for it, sunny weather or long winters?
- What is the oldest part of your house? What is the newest part?

A note on timing: If people are really engaged in telling about their house, and the others are listening intently and responding well, you can let this part of the session go on for forty minutes or more. If members of the group have made an effort to draw this metaphorical house, then this exercise generally proves to be one of the most memorable of the sessions.

An Exploration of Christian Faith Practices   00:50
(30 minutes)

Hand out the list of Christian faith practices (page 53) and explain:

- Over the history of Christianity, these are some ways that people have intentionally 'practiced' their faith. Some people speak of yoga as a practice, or meditation as a practice.
- Christian faith and Christian life also rest upon, and are embodied by, Christian practices. We might think of Christian practices as ways in which we "build up our house of faith."

Review the list of practices and ask people which practice means the most to them in their life of faith, and why.

Typical Christian Practices[7]

1. *Worship:* Gathering to praise God, hear the Word read and preached, and receive the sacraments.
2. *Sharing the Story:* Reading and studying scripture, teaching in church, learning about the history of the church.
3. *Prayer:* Alone and with others, privately in devotional time, publicly in worship, at all times and in all places.
4. *Confession/Forgiving/Reconciling:* Working to own our faults, make peace with those we have hurt, forgive those who hurt us and to live as reconciled people.
5. *Acts of Service and Witness:* Doing acts of charity, serving the community, publicly identifying that work as part of being a Christian.
6. *Giving:* Time, talent, and treasure to share what we have been given with others.
7. *Striving for Justice and Peace:* Working to make the world more like the dream of God by resisting unjust structures, striving to create places of equity for all, building peace in our homes, our community, and the world.
8. *Caring for Creation:* Being mindful of our call as stewards of the earth, by tending, recycling, repairing, and respecting the created world.

---

7. This list of practices is a compilation that draws on other lists developed by the Valparaiso Project on the Education and Formation of People in Faith, Baylor University School of Social Work, and Diana Butler Bass.

9. *Hospitality:* Graciously opening our hearts, homes, churches, and lives to others. Welcoming each person as if he or she were Christ himself.
10. *Honoring the Body:* Caring for our bodies and minds, practicing balance in food and drink, being good stewards of our sexuality.

Explain to the group that practices are how we put our faith in motion.

* Adopting certain practices can help strengthen your faith. They can also help you visibly live out your faith in your daily life.
* Which of these practices do you think you might want to focus on more intentionally and why?

You can take the conversation deeper with the following questions:

* Are there things you will never do because you are a Christian? Are there things you must do because you are a Christian? Is your life (or choices or path) different from your peers' because of your faith? or not?
* How can you tell a Christian from someone who is just a "good person"? What is the biggest challenge for you in living out your faith?

The Final Assignment: Your Statement of Faith   01:20
(5 minutes)

Distribute the Baptismal Covenant handout (page 54). Explain that the Episcopal Church presents the commitment of baptism as a two-part statement: First, the Apostles' Creed, which describes God in the ways that the 2,000-year tradition of Christianity has understood God. And then, the five questions, which explain what is required of us to be in relationship with this God, as a child of this God.

Explain to the group that the final exercise is to write a personal covenant statement. Flip the handout over and read the two parts:

WHO IS GOD?

What can you say about God, your understanding of who God is . . . today . . . knowing that any description of God can only be partial—and always culturally and personally contextual—but in a description that is *yours*?

And then . . .

WHAT IS REQUIRED OF YOU AS A PERSON IN RELATIONSHIP WITH THIS GOD?
As a child of this God, or a follower of this God, or as a beloved
of this God? What practices, commandments, moral imperatives, or commitments does this relationship require of you?

In a sense, this assignment is the capstone of the sessions, the chance
for each participant to articulate for themselves a statement of belief
and practice. The intention in this assignment is to help each participant
be able to speak their own truth, giving voice to the many ideas, questions, clarifications, and images that have circulated among them over
the preceding sessions.

Ask them to return with their covenant statement for the final session.

Closing Prayer   01:25
(5 minutes)

Use the prayer practice you have been using in previous sessions.

This I Believe

This session is the culmination of the five weeks. The "Your Statement of Faith" exercise gives participants a chance to articulate their own theology and ethics based on the Baptismal Covenant. Before they share their statements, it's worthwhile to reflect on the process of developing the statements. How did participating in the conversations help with writing this statement? What did the process do in terms of helping them own an articulated faith?

The process of sharing the statements is the centerpiece of the session, and group members should be given time to reflect on and respond to one another's statements. After the statements have been thoroughly shared, reflect on what they can say now that they couldn't have said five weeks prior.

A final question about what is the "good news" or what is life-changing for each of them in their relationship with God helps them to think about how they might articulate their faith to others as they go forward. It is also helpful to surface questions and ideas that didn't get resolved during the sessions and to think about what each person needs to do next to continue to grow in faith. In this session, participants articulate their state of faith to one another and begin to reflect on the next stage of their spiritual journeys.

Opening Prayer   00:00
(5 minutes)

As this is the concluding session, it is appropriate for you as the leader to pray for the members of your group and their ongoing and on-growing life in Christ. Tell them you are going to use the prayer for the baptismal candidates from the Book of Common Prayer to encourage them in living out their baptismal life. Their response is "Lord, hear our prayer."

> Deliver them, O Lord, from the way of sin and death. *Lord, hear our prayer.*
> Open their hearts to your grace and truth. *Lord, hear our prayer.*

Fill them with your Holy and Life-giving Spirit. *Lord, hear our prayer.*

Keep them in the faith and communion of your holy Church. *Lord, hear our prayer.*

Teach them to love others in the power of the Spirit. *Lord, hear our prayer.*

Send them into the world in witness to your love. *Lord, hear our prayer.*

Bring them to the fullness of your peace and glory. *Lord, hear our prayer.*

Amen.

Discuss the Assignment   00:05

(10 minutes)

Debrief the assignment as a group before each participant shares their statement. Begin with:

* So you had this final assignment about thinking about God and what your response to God should be. And I wonder how was the experience of actually doing this kind of thinking? For all of you, before you get to the sheet itself, how was it working through that?
* Was it easy or was it hard? What did you struggle with? What came clear?

Other follow-up questions:

* Who wants to go next?
* What was this like for you?
* Were there places where the traditions of our faith were helpful to you in doing this or places where you struggled with them?
* What did you learn about yourself by doing this exercise?

Sharing the Statements   00:15

(30 minutes)

When everyone has had a chance to comment on the experience, invite people to share the statements they actually wrote. There is not commentary yet from other members of the group. Each person is given time to read their statement fully and freely.

Each person should read whatever they came up with for their statements. When they finish reading, your best response is, "Thank you. Who wants to go next?" Always say "thank you." When everyone is done, be sure to say "Thank you. All of you."

Conclude:

- I hope everybody feels like this is your statement of faith for you who you are, where you are today.
- You may do it again in a year and it would be changed, or not, but it's yours. It's your words and it's your relationship with God and your understanding that you just articulated.

Processing the Experience   00:45
(30 minutes)

Now it's time for questions and discussion. Ask:

- How was this experience of reading your faith statement aloud?
- What do you think you can say better about God than what you could say five weeks ago? Where are you still working on it?
- What have you learned from the other members of the group?
- What is the Good News—for you—in your understanding of God?
- If you were going to talk to someone about your faith outside of church, what would you say about the state of your faith?
- What have you learned about speaking? What have you learned about listening?
- Where was God in this process for you? Did you experience God in these sessions? What was that like? What are you taking away from these conversations? What questions still linger?

The Final Challenge   1:15
(15 minutes)

Remind them:

- The final gathering of this program is not today, but one month from now. We will come back together for a celebration: to catch up with one another's lives, to reconnect with the energy and passion we felt in this group, but most importantly, we will gather to share the outcome of our final challenge.

- What is a good day and time for us to get back together?

Have the group set the date and time and nature of the celebration now. There is more information about the final celebration in the next section of this guide. Give them an idea of the ways and styles you all might use to regroup in a few weeks. If your group has gone well, they may be chomping at the bit to figure out how to be together again, and soon.

When you have the date and time settled, it's time to explain the final challenge:

- The purpose of Speaking Our Faith is to help all of us get better at talking about faith. It has helped each of you become more aware of what you actually believe, and what is the nature of your own faith journey. And talking about it in this group has helped you practice and get more competent at talking about faith with other people.
- This is part of the Jesus Movement, to share the good news of a loving God with others. So here is the final Speaking Our Faith Challenge: between now and our final celebration, sometime in the next few weeks, have a conversation about faith with someone you *know already*, but who does not share your faith. This is not meant to be a time for converting someone, but for practicing the skills you have developed in respectful listening, thoughtful inquiry, and speaking your own truth.

Ask who they think they might want to talk to. It cannot be another Christian, but a person of any other faith (or absence of faith) is eligible. Give them some ideas: Do they have a friend of a different faith than Christianity they could talk to in an interfaith/cultural exchange? Is there someone very close to them whom they would like to have know that God is important to them? Who might be intrigued to hear about this Speaking Our Faith journey that they have been experiencing?

Brainstorm some low-pressure ways of having a conversation with people they already know and feel comfortable with. This is not supposed to be a sell job or an attempt at conversion. This is just a chance to try having a faith conversation outside the safety of the group, with other people whom they know.

Closing Prayer   1:30
(5 minutes)

Before you end with your usual prayer, invite each person to pray for the person on their right as you go around the circle. From everything they have heard, all the ways they have gotten to know the person on their right, what would they like to offer up in prayer for that person? Then conclude with your usual prayer.

One Month Later

As the leader, you sent the members of your Speaking Our Faith group out at the end of the last session with a mission: *Have a conversation about faith with someone you know who does not share your faith.* The participants should know as they go that this is just supposed to be a conversation, not a sales pitch, and not a sell job. Just talking with someone they already know—a friend, a colleague, a family member.

Now it's time for your group to come together one last time, to report back on the outcomes of this conversational challenge. You hope they will return with joy, like the seventy disciples in the tenth chapter of Luke's gospel after their first missionary outing. And even if they did not find that demons submitted to them in Jesus's name, they should have ventured to have at least one conversation about faith with another person.

During the closing of Session Five, your group should have agreed on a date to get together again, about a month later. Many Speaking Our Faith groups really bond, and the members will likely be looking forward to getting together again. Plan that this gathering will be a celebration, done in a way that suits your group's temperament. You may want to gather at a participant's home for a meal. You may want to return to your usual meeting space with a catered spread—anything from bagels and coffee to Thai food. Or a dessert gathering, build your own sundae, perhaps. Or a potluck. Whatever you plan, it should feel festive, like a reunion and a celebration.

Of course, begin this special session with prayer, with grace over the food, or with prayers of gratitude for the group and for this reunion. Then use the refreshment time as a check-in time. Each participant can simply say what has been going on in his or her life over the past few weeks. This may happen completely naturally—a group that has already spent this much time together will probably have plenty to say to one another. Or you can prime the pump after everyone gets settled with their plates.

- Let's do a check-in, just to catch up with where we've been in the last few weeks.
- Who would like to start?

Remind the group of its norms, particularly around listening to each person with intention, and give everyone a chance to say what they need to say to check in.

After the social time is over, and after checking in, it's time to find out how the conversations went.

Sharing and Closure

You can use a short introductory script to get them started:

- You left the group last time with a challenge. To have a conversation about faith with someone you know who does not share your faith. And then to come back together today to share how those conversations went.
- Was everyone able to have a conversation with someone?

If some individuals did not have a conversation, that is OK. Invite them to talk about their thought process:

- Who did they want to talk to? Why didn't that happen?
- Are they still going to try, or has the moment passed? Have they talked to anyone about faith in the intervening weeks?

But lead off the discussion with someone who did complete the conversation challenge, and let anyone who did not complete the challenge fill in as you go. Ask the group who would like to go first, and say:

- Tell us who you talked to, and why.
- And how did the conversation go?

As their description of the conversation unfolds, you can use any of these prompts to go deeper:

- What was it like for you to have this conversation?
- What did the conversation entail?
- Did anything that happened in our group connect to this conversation?
- Did you draw on any of the exercises we did?

- Did you notice any difference in your comfort level around talking about faith?
- Do you think you will talk to anyone else about faith going forward?

The other members of the group may have questions to ask too, and that is fine. Just be sure you leave enough time for each person to tell their story. As you watch the clock, you may have to move on to someone else, by saying something affirming like: "That was a courageous thing for you to do." "That sounds like a really interesting conversation." "Good for you for reaching out to that person." But then say, "We should move on to the next person so everyone gets a chance to share."

You may find that these conversations were really hard for your group members. Maybe they talked to someone very close to them who really does not believe—a spouse, child, or parent. Or the conversations might have been energizing and stimulating, if they had a dialogue across faith traditions and learned something new about themselves and the other person, about being a Muslim or a Hindu, or even an atheist. Or the conversation may have stumbled along, and the group member may feel bad that it didn't go as they had hoped. Your job as facilitator is to really affirm the courage and vulnerability it took for these people to engage with this challenge. Remind them that talking with their fellow group members in a safe space is very different from initiating a conversation with someone. Honor their bravery. And for anyone who didn't manage to have this kind of conversation, be encouraging—they *will* be able to talk to someone, going forward.

It will be helpful for the group, and for you as the facilitator, to take some time at the end to process this entire experience. Ask the group how they feel about their Speaking Our Faith journey:

- What have they learned about their own faith?
- How have they changed or not changed in their desire to talk about faith?
- Has anything shifted for them?
- Do they think they will have more conversations with people about God or church or faith going forward? Why or why not?

This is the last time your group will be together like this. They may want to continue to meet for support, conversation, and friendship. This may be the beginning of a "Jesus Movement" group in your congregation that really wants to start talking about faith to others. If they want to continue, you may decide to be part of the group's future shape, or you can set them free to figure out their own collective life as they move out from this experience. Whatever is going to happen next, end this session with a liturgy or time of prayer that brings closure to their life together as this Speaking Our Faith group. Be sure you have spent some time thinking and planning the closing liturgy before this session, so that it is planned and intentional.

This Ending Is For You, Too

And so, the members of your Speaking Our Faith group leave, and you realize that this has all come to its inevitable ending. I know from my own experience leading Speaking Our Faith groups, and from following up with others who have facilitated these groups, that this experience can deeply affect you. You have been walking through tender, vulnerable questions with these people as they engaged with their own understanding of God and relationship with God. These questions probably touched you as well, affecting your own understanding of God and relationship with God.

As the group facilitator, how are you feeling about this experience? This has been a journey of faith for you as well. Perhaps you learned something about touch points in your own life with God, questions you still have about the nature of God and how that relates to your walk of faith. You probably learned about yourself as a facilitator of conversations. Maybe some of the people in your group proved to be difficult, shy, or unwilling, and you had to work to draw them out and include them in the discussions. Or some may have tried to dominate the conversations and you needed to divert their engagement to make room for others to speak. How did you navigate the dynamics of this particular constellation of people over the past five weeks? What do you walk away with from this experience?

I encourage you to do some writing and reflecting on your own about your Speaking Our Faith journey. If you are a regular journal-keeper, take some journaling time to explore how you have grown and changed through this process. If you don't journal, you can still take some time apart and write your story of this Speaking our Faith experience as a single reflection. Start with simple questions:

- What did I learn?
- Where did I grow?
- How was I challenged?
- What moved me?

- Where did I find God in this experience?
- How do I speak about faith in my own life? Did that change because of this group? Did the shape of my faith change?
- Who was I when I started the group? Who am I right now?

We follow a loving, liberating, life-giving God, who wants to draw all people into relationship with that self-same God, and who wants to transform this world into the dream God has always had for the world. You have been part of this movement of love, liberation, and life for these past few weeks. Your leadership has helped others to deepen their relationship with God. Your leadership has helped them to accept that faith can make them feel vulnerable, and that they don't have all the answers about God, and that's OK. They can still learn to speak their own truth to a world that desperately needs to hear good news of a loving God.

And now your group members—and you, too—are better equipped to respond to Jesus's call to us in the Great Commission, to go into the world and make disciples of all people. Your group members—and you, too—should now be able to respond boldly, even joyfully, to that question in the Baptismal Covenant: "Will you proclaim by word and example the Good News of God in Christ?"

May they respond . . . may you respond . . . may all of us respond, with a new hope and a new desire: "I will, with God's help."

CIRCLES OF FAITH

STAGES OF FAITH
Based on the work of John Westerhoff in *Will Our Children Have Faith?* (1976)

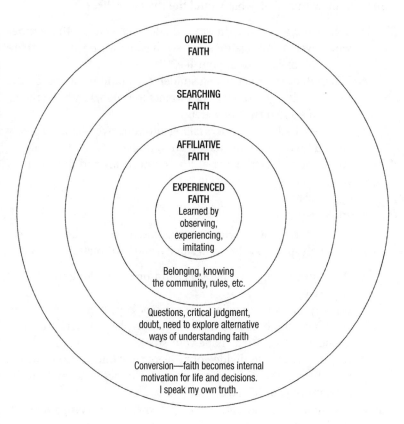

OWNED
FAITH

SEARCHING
FAITH

AFFILIATIVE
FAITH

EXPERIENCED
FAITH
Learned by
observing,
experiencing,
imitating

Belonging, knowing
the community, rules, etc.

Questions, critical judgment,
doubt, need to explore alternative
ways of understanding faith

Conversion—faith becomes internal
motivation for life and decisions.
I speak my own truth.

HANDOUT B

RIVER OF LIFE: A LIFE REVIEW ACTIVITY[8]

Begin with a blank sheet of paper. Before you put anything on the paper, think briefly about the course of your whole life. If you were able to compare your life with a river, what would the river look like?

- When and where are the smooth, flowing waters—those times when events and relationships seem generally positive or there is a sense of ease about your life?
- When does the river take a sudden turn (and what caused the turn), or change from smooth waters to rough, tumbling rapids or to an excited rush of water?
- Are there rocks or boulders falling into your river—unexpectedly landed there, changing its direction forever?
- Are there points at which it flows powerfully and purposefully or seems to slow to a trickle?

Instructions

A. Draw your river of life with its bends and turns, its smooth waters and rough spots, its strength/vitality, and its direction.

- Write in your approximate age, and/or dates, along the flow of your river.
- Identify on your drawing the various key "marker events" in your life—the boulders in the river, or places where the river changes course—that shape your story.
- If you were able to divide your life journey into sections, where would the section divisions occur? Give names to each of the sections of your life river.

B. Now think about the various people who have accompanied you along this river's journey.

---

8. Taken from *Girl Talk/God Talk: Why Faith Matters to Teenage Girls—and Their Parents* by Joyce Ann Mercer, Copyright 2008 by John Wiley & Sons. Reproduced with permission of John Wiley & Sons.

- What relationships have been the most significant at different points in your life?
- Who has most shaped you?
- Have there been significant losses of relationship along the way?
- What groups or communities of people were most important?
- Record these key relationships and losses in the appropriate places on your river of life.
- If you wish, you might also want to jot down some of the thoughts and feelings that go along with these relationships.

C. As you look over the diagram of your life river, think about the different ways you have experienced and understood God across your life.

- Who or what was God to you at the different times depicted in your diagram?
- What caused you to feel closer to, or more distant from, God at these different times?
- What places or situations were encounters with the Sacred for you?
- Have you faced situations or experiences devoid of any sense of God/the Sacred?
- Decide on a way to note these matters, with words and/or symbols, and place them into your river.

D. In relation to your life's journey:

- Are there times of significant pain or suffering—yours or others'—that shape the flow of your life river?
- What has happened along the journey of your life that you associate with evil?
- Add these elements to your river.

E. Rivers do not exist in isolation but are always part of a larger ecology. So, too, is human life situated in a larger world.

- What was going on in the world—local, regional, and world events—that shaped the flow of your river?
- Using words and/or symbols, place these events in the appropriate locations on your river.

F. As you reflect on your river of life,

- What values, commitments, causes, or principles were most important to you at a given point in your life?

- Toward what goals, if any, were your primary energies directed—or, metaphorically speaking, what purposes and ends helped to shape the flow of life waters at a given time in your experience?
- Note these on your river.

Taking a Step Back

As you finish depicting your river of life, take a look over the whole diagram.

- Do its symbols and words seem to portray how you think and feel about the whole of your life?
- Is there some important element left out?
- Make adjustments as needed. Remember that no drawing can possibly capture all that shapes a person's journey. This is intended to be a beginning point for reflection and/or conversation, not a comprehensive depiction of your life!

TYPICAL CHRISTIAN PRACTICES

1. *Worship:* Gathering to praise God, hear the Word read and preach, receive the sacraments.
2. *Sharing the Story:* Reading and studying scripture, teaching in church, learning about the history of the church.
3. *Prayer:* Alone and with others, privately in devotional time, publicly in worship, at all times and in all places.
4. *Confession/Forgiving/Reconciling:* Working to own our faults, make peace with those we have hurt, forgive those who hurt us and to live as reconciled people.
5. *Acts of Service and Witness:* Doing acts of charity, serving the community, publicly identifying that work as part of being a Christian.
6. *Giving:* Time, talent, and treasure to share what we have been given with others.
7. *Striving for Justice and Peace:* Working to make the world more like the dream of God by resisting unjust structures, striving to create places of equity for all, building peace in our homes, our community, and the world.
8. *Caring for Creation:* Being mindful of our call as stewards of the earth, by tending, recycling, repairing, and respecting the created world.
9. *Hospitality:* Graciously opening our hearts, homes, churches, and lives to others. Welcoming each person as if he or she were Christ himself.
10. *Honoring the Body:* Caring for our bodies and minds, practicing balance in food and drink, being good stewards of our sexuality.

HANDOUT D

THE BAPTISMAL COVENANT[9]

(This begins with the Apostles' Creed, an ancient statement of faith about the Triune God. It says basically who we believe the God we are in relationship with is.)

Celebrant	Do you believe in God the Father?
People	I believe in God, the Father almighty,
	creator of heaven and earth.

Celebrant	Do you believe in Jesus Christ, the Son of God?
People	I believe in Jesus Christ, his only Son, our Lord.
	He was conceived by the power of the Holy Spirit
	and born of the Virgin Mary.
	He suffered under Pontius Pilate,
	was crucified, died, and was buried.
	He descended to the dead.
	On the third day he rose again.
	He ascended into heaven,
	and is seated at the right hand of the Father.
	He will come again to judge the living and the dead.

Celebrant	Do you believe in God the Holy Spirit?
People	I believe in the Holy Spirit,
	the holy catholic Church,
	the communion of saints,
	the forgiveness of sins,
	the resurrection of the body,
	and the life everlasting.

---

9. The Book of Common Prayer, 304–305.

(Five questions outline the Episcopal Church's late twentieth–century understanding of what it means to live a life in relationship with the Triune God . . . what is required of us when we become part of God's family in baptism.)

Celebrant	Will you continue in the apostles' teaching and fellowship, in the breaking of bread, and in the prayers?
People	I will, with God's help.
Celebrant	Will you persevere in resisting evil, and, whenever you fall into sin, repent and return to the Lord?
People	I will, with God's help.
Celebrant	Will you proclaim by word and example the Good News of God in Christ?
People	I will, with God's help.
Celebrant	Will you seek and serve Christ in all persons, loving your neighbor as yourself?
People	I will, with God's help.
Celebrant	Will you strive for justice and peace among all people, and respect the dignity of every human being?
People	I will, with God's help.

(Book of Common Prayer, pp. 304–305, circa 1979.)

YOUR OWN OUTLINE OF FAITH

Who is God?

(What can you say about God, your understanding of who God is, today, knowing that any description of God can only be partial—and always culturally and personally contextual—but in a description that is yours?)

What is required of you as a person in relationship with this God?

(As a child of this God, or a follower of this God, or as a beloved of this God? What practices, commandments, moral imperatives, or commitments does this relationship require of you?)